THE EARLY TUDOR CH

The Early Tudor Church and Society, 1485–1529

John A. F. Thomson

Longman
LONDON AND NEW YORK

Longman Group UK Limited,
Longman House, Burnt Mill,
Harlow, Essex CM20 2JE, England
and Associated Companies throughout the world.

Published in the United States of America
by Longman Publishing, New York

© Longman Group UK Limited 1993

First published 1993

ISBN 0–582–21872–1 CSD
ISBN 0–582–06377–9 PPR

British Library Cataloguing-in-Publication Data

A catalogue record for this book is
available from the British Library

Library of Congress Cataloging in Publication Data
Thomson, John A. F.
 The early Tudor church and society, 1485–1529 / John A. F. Thomson.
  p. cm.
 Includes bibliographical references and index.
 ISBN 0–582–21872–1 (CSD). — ISBN 0–582–06377–9 (PPR)
1. England—Church history—16th century. 2. Church and state—
England—History—16th century. 3. Catholic Church—England—
History—Modern period, 1500– I. Title.
BR755.T54 1993   92–33484
274.2′05—dc20   CIP

Set by 5 in Bembo

Produced by Longman Singapore Publishers (Pte) Ltd.
Printed in Singapore

Contents